GET ACTIVE!

BUILDING STRENGTH

Written by Valerie Harvey

KidHaven PUBLISHING

Published in 2027 by
KidHaven Publishing, an Imprint of Greenhaven Publishing, LLC
2544 Clinton St., Buffalo, NY 14224

Written by: Valerie Harvey
Edited by: Elise Carraway
Designed by: Amy Li

Cataloging-in-Publication Data

Names: Harvey, Valerie.
Title: Building strength / Valerie Harvey.
Description: Buffalo, NY : KidHaven Publishing, 2027. | Series: Get active! | Includes glossary and index.
Identifiers: ISBN 9781534570795 (pbk.) | ISBN 9781534570801 (library bound) | ISBN 9781534570818 (ebook)
Subjects: LCSH: Weight training--Juvenile literature. | Isometric exercise--Juvenile literature. | Muscle strength--Juvenile literature.
Classification: LCC GV546.2 H378 2027 | DDC 613.713--dc23

Printed in China

CPSIA compliance information: Batch #QS27KH: For further information contact Greenhaven Publishing LLC at 1-844-317-7404.

Please visit our website, www.greenhavenpublishing.com.
For a free color catalog of all our high-quality books, call toll free 1-844-317-7404 or fax 1-844-317-7405.

Find us on

Image Credits. All images are courtesy of Shutterstock.com, unless otherwise stated.

Recurring – Tatiana Kubara, VVadi4ka. Cover – Ahturner. 2–3 – BAZA Production. 4–5 – Ladanifer, TinnaPong. 6–7 – alphaspirit.it, Anatoliy Karlyuk. 8–9 – ivector, Rawpixel.com, RAVINDU99PICS. 10–11 – Evan Lorne, Tatjana Baibakova. 12–13 – wavebreakmedia, WHYFRAME. 14–15 – Sergey Novikov, Zulfiska. 16–17 – BAZA Production, FOTO Eak. 18–19 – pics five. 20–21 – Sorapop Udomsri, VisanuPhotoshop. 22–23 – AYO Production, Divin Serhiy, smilepoker.

CONTENTS

Words that look like this can be found in the glossary on page 24.

WE CAN GET ACTIVE!

You can get active by moving your body to have fun and stay healthy. Getting active means doing things such as running, jumping, playing, and exercising to keep your body strong and full of energy.

Using your strength is part of getting active. It is important to know about what your muscles need and how to keep them strong and healthy. Let's get moving and discover what your body can do!

WHAT IS STRENGTH?

Strength means having a strong body that helps you move around, lift things, and carry things. Strength comes from using your muscles. Playing outside, riding your bicycle, and playing sports can all build strength.

Strength is important in sports. It helps athletes run faster, jump higher, and throw farther. Having strong muscles is also important for everyday life. Strong muscles help people avoid getting hurt.

MUSCLES

Muscles are the parts of our bodies that help us move. When you move, your muscles work by stretching and relaxing. They are a bit like rubber bands that help your whole body move.

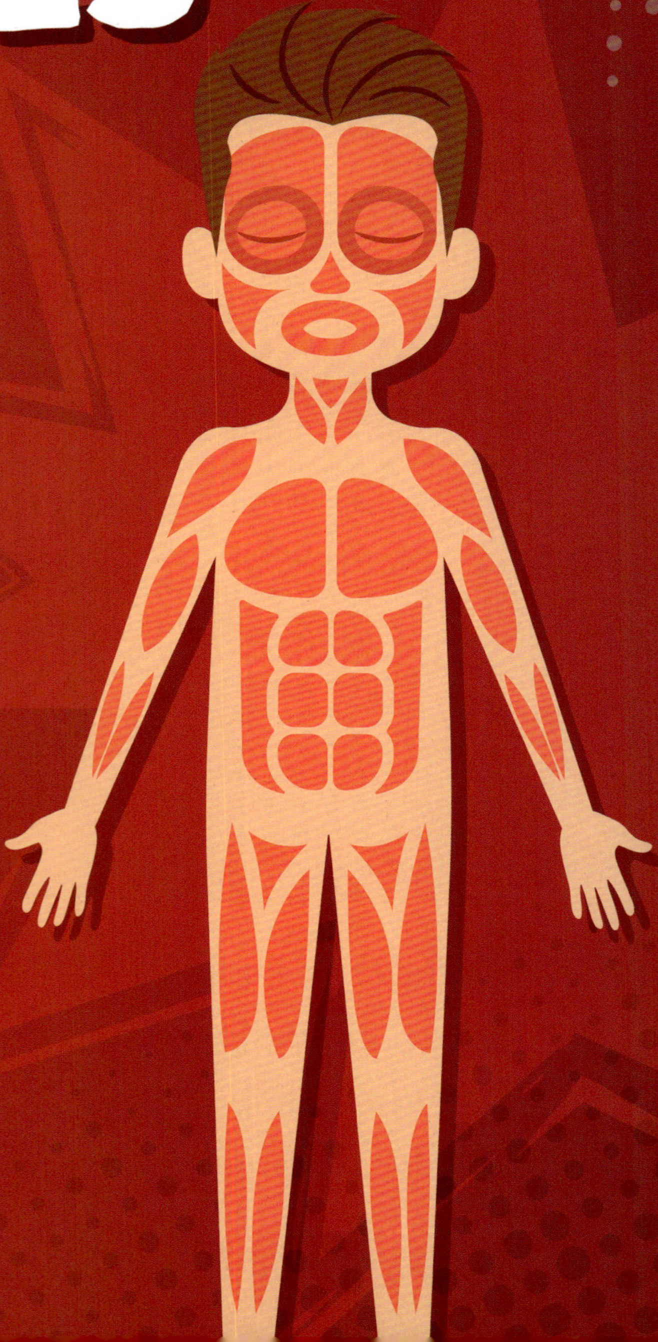

The more you use your muscles, the stronger they get. This makes it easier to climb, dance, and lift things. Athletes work hard to keep their muscles strong and healthy by using them often.

DIET

Your diet is all the things you usually eat. It is important to eat a balanced diet. Eating different foods in the right amounts makes sure your body gets everything it needs to stay healthy.

Athletes eat a balanced diet to stay strong and perform well. Many athletes get extra protein by eating high-protein foods. Protein helps your muscles get bigger and stronger after exercise.

Foods such as meat, eggs, beans, nuts, and seeds are good sources of protein.

WARMING UP AND COOLING DOWN

Warming up your muscles gets your body ready to move. This is like gently waking your muscles up. Cooling down after exercise helps your body ease back to normal.

Gentle movement and stretching help warm your muscles up.

Warming up and cooling down help stop your muscles from hurting. It is also important to make sure you give your muscles plenty of rest.

PUSH AND PULL

When you exercise, pushing means using your muscles to move something away from your body. A push-up is an exercise that uses pushing to build strength.

Pulling is when you use your muscles to bring something closer. You use pulling movements when you are lifting something or doing a pull-up. Doing pushing and pulling movements balances the exercise your muscles get.

TRAINING

Strength training is a type of exercise that helps your muscles grow stronger. It also helps build endurance. It includes fun movements such as lifting weights and using resistance bands.

Professional athletes do lots of strength training to keep their bodies strong and healthy. When strength training, it is important to start with light weights. Using weights that are too heavy can cause injuries.

Strength training also helps keep your bones healthy.

HIGH-INTENSITY EXERCISES

It can be fun to exercise by doing short bursts of fast movements, such as jumping jacks or running, then resting for a little bit. These kinds of activities are high-intensity exercises.

High-intensity activities can help your heart, muscles, and lungs get stronger. It is a fun way to keep active and healthy. However, it is important to be careful. Do not push yourself too hard doing high-intensity activities.

STAYING SAFE

When using sports equipment, it is important to use it safely. We should always use equipment the right way and listen carefully to rules. This keeps you and everyone around you safe.

You might need to wear a helmet, elbow pads, or knee pads for some sports.

You should also be very careful when using weights to exercise. Lifting heavy things helps you get stronger. But make sure you are not lifting anything too heavy!

Check with an adult before lifting any weights.

SUPER STRENGTH!

Some adults, such as construction workers or firefighters, need to be strong to do their jobs. Through exercise, they train their muscles to become strong enough to lift heavy things and do tough tasks.

Some athletes use their strength to help them win competitions. Many people build their strength because they enjoy training and want to stay healthy.

What would you like to do with your strength?

GLOSSARY

ATHLETES people who are skilled at sports

ENDURANCE the ability to keep going without giving up

ENERGY the power that makes living things able to move and live

PROTEIN something found in certain kinds of foods that helps the muscles grow strong and healthy

RESISTANCE BANDS stretchy bands that can be pulled and stretched to exercise with

INDEX